This short book packs a punch! Tim Chester tackles our questions about miracles honestly and biblically, challenges our assumptions, and leads us to a God who is even bigger than we imagined.

Elizabeth McQuoid,
Writer and Commissioning Editor, Keswick Ministries

In an area of great confusion, Tim Chester provides compelling arguments and clear guidance. Thoughtful, careful and caring, this little book will be immensely helpful to all who read it.

Graham Beynon,
Minister, Grace Church, Cambridge;
Director of Independent Ministry, Oak Hill College, London

Tim Chester has written a profoundly helpful book on miracles. As a pastor I am frequently asked if we should pray for miracles, why we don't see more of them, and what to do when God doesn't grant a miracle. This book answers all of these questions—but it does more. Its compelling focus on Jesus orders miracles beneath the Miracle-worker himself in a way I've not seen before. Refreshing, insightful, thought-provoking and hand-out worthy!

Jonathan Dodson,
Lead pastor, City Life Church, Austin, Texas

Do miracles happen today?

And other questions about signs,
wonders and mighty works

Tim Chester

Do miracles happen today?
And other questions about signs, wonders and mighty works
Part of the *Questions Christians Ask* series
© Tim Chester, 2020.

Published by:
The Good Book Company

thegoodbook.com | thegoodbook.co.uk
thegoodbook.com.au | thegoodbook.co.nz | thegoodbook.co.in

Unless indicated, all Scripture references are taken from the Holy Bible, New International Version. Copyright © 2011 Biblica. Used by permission.

A CIP catalogue record for this book is available from the British Library.

ISBN: 9781909559691 | Printed in India

Design by André Parker

Contents

"Jesus of Nazareth was a man accredited by God to you by miracles, wonders and signs"

Acts 2 v 22

Can my friend be healed?

As we sat together in the staff canteen, she told me that her best friend was dying of cancer. She was full of a sense of the loss that was coming, unsure of how she would cope.

But Christians in her church had told her that her friend would be healed if only she had faith. At first that had sounded like good news. Here was hope. She had prayed. Both of them had prayed. The whole church had prayed. And on some days, the good days, it looked as if maybe God had heard those prayers—as if things were on the up. Perhaps the cancer was in retreat. Perhaps the tumour was shrinking. But the bad days were overtaking the good days. It was becoming clear that her friend's condition was getting worse. Was it her fault? Was her friend paying the price of her faltering faith? Or did God not care?

"What do you think?" she asked me. "Do miracles happen today? Can my friend be healed?"

Chapter 1

Did miracles happen then?

Lots of weird stuff happens in the Bible. People walk on water. People touch handkerchiefs and are healed. People disappear into the sky. (Matthew 14 v 22-33; Acts 19 v 11-12; 2 Kings 2 v 11-12; Acts 1 v 9) These events stretch credibility. And at different points people have asked me, "How can you believe in such far-fetched stories?" and "How can you take the miracles of the Bible seriously in the light of modern science?"

Our lack of experience doesn't rule out miracles

The 18th-century Scottish philosopher, David Hume, says this about miracles:

Nothing is esteemed a miracle, if it ever happens in the common course of nature ... There must, therefore, be a uniform experience against every miraculous event, otherwise the event would not merit that appellation. And as a uniform experience amounts to a proof, there is here a

direct and full proof, from the nature of the fact,
against the existence of any miracle.[1]

What Hume is saying is this: by definition, a miracle is an event outside normal human experience—otherwise it's not a miracle. But if it's outside our experience, then we must doubt its existence because we've never seen it.

It is said the King of Siam refused to believe stories of rivers that became so hard that elephants could walk across them. Nothing in his experience prepared him for such a possibility. You can sympathise with his incredulity. But the fact that he had never encountered ice does not mean ice does not exist, nor that rivers never freeze over.[2]

The experience of our generation can't be the criterion for what can happen. Just because you've never seen a miracle doesn't mean a miracle can't happen. Elsewhere, Hume himself says we can't prove that "the future must be conformable to the past".[3]

The laws of nature don't rule out miracles

Hume has another argument against miracles: "A miracle is a violation of the laws of nature; and as a firm and unalterable experience has established these laws, the proof against a miracle, from the very nature of the

---

1   David Hume, *An Enquiry Concerning Human Understanding* (1748), ed. L. A. Selby-Bigge (1894), Section 10, Part 1, p 114-5.

2   Colin Brown, *Miracles and the Critical Mind* (Paternoster, 1984), p 84.

3   David Hume, *An Abstract of A Treatise on Human Nature* (1740), ed. John Maynard Keynes and Piero Sraffa (1938), p 15.

fact, is as entire as any argument from experience can possibly be imagined". In other words, miracles violate the laws of nature and we know that can't happen.

C.S. Lewis, the Oxford professor who wrote the Narnia Chronicles, once gave this illustration. Suppose I put £2 in a drawer. Then a week later I add another £2 and the following week a further £2. Suppose I then open my drawer and discover only £1. What has happened? Have the laws of arithmetic been broken or the laws of England?

His point was twofold. First, the laws of nature are not like the laws of England. We're using the word "law" in a different sense. The laws of nature are not statutes that must be obeyed, but patterns we observe in the world around us. "There are not such laws [of nature]," says the Scottish author Donald Macleod. "There are only customs of God, describing the way that he normally preserves and governs the world of created reality, in all its fullness and variety."[4] The English theologian John Stott is not as hostile to the terminology, but makes the same point: "Natural law is not an alternative to divine action, but a useful way of referring to it. So-called 'natural' laws simply describe the uniformity which scientists have observed."[5]

Our formulae and principles *describe* the patterns we see. But scientists are not police enforcing the laws of nature. They're people who are gradually discerning

---

4   Donald Macleod, *Behold Your God* (Christian Focus, 1995), p 80.

5   John Stott, *"But I Say to You": Christ the Controversialist* (IVP UK, 2013), p 54.

and discovering the patterns of the world. The very language of "laws" of nature comes from Christian scientists who assumed that the patterns they observed in the world around them had been placed there by a divine law-giver. If there is a God who intervenes in our world, he's not bound by the laws of nature as if they're some decree.

Second, what has happened when C.S. Lewis only finds £1 in the drawer? Almost certainly there has been "an intervention". Someone has opened the drawer and stolen some money. Has the thief violated the laws of arithmetic? No. It's not that they've made $2 + 2 + 2 = 1$. Instead, they've simply stolen £5. They've changed the calculation so that it has become $2 + 2 + 2 - 5 = 1$. In the same way, if there is a God and if he intervenes from outside our universe, he's not "violating" the laws of nature. He's simply changing the context in which they operate. If there is a Creator, then there's no law which says he can't intervene in his world to perform miracles. "It would be ridiculous to suppose," says John Stott, "that the creation now controls the Creator. He is able to step aside from his uniformity, and the Bible says that he has sometimes done so."[6]

Test case: the resurrection

So there's no reason to suppose miracles *can't* happen. But, of course, that doesn't mean they do. It certainly doesn't mean every miraculous claim is true. It's right

---

6   John Stott, *"But I Say to You": Christ the Controversialist* (IVP UK, 2013), p 56.

to be sceptical. Something can be possible in theory without being true in practice. It might be theoretically possible that there's life on Mars. But, as far as we know, that doesn't mean there is. So let's consider another question: *do miracles happen?*

The resurrection of Jesus is the key miracle for Christian faith. Christianity stands or falls by this miracle. If God can bring life where there is no life, then nothing is impossible for him. Walking on water is still weird, but it is possible for a God who can raise the dead. The Bible itself says, "If Christ has not been raised, your faith is futile; you are still in your sins" (1 Corinthians 15 v 17). You can take other miracles out of the Bible and the Christian faith would still be coherent. But if you disprove this miracle, then the whole thing comes crashing down. Again, let me quote David Hume: "The Christian religion not only was at first attended with miracles, but even at this day cannot be believed by any reasonable person without one".

Here's the apostle John's account of the resurrection from John 20:

> On the evening of that first day of the week, when the disciples were together, with the doors locked for fear of the Jewish leaders, Jesus came and stood among them and said, "Peace be with you!" After he said this, he showed them his hands and side. The disciples were overjoyed when they saw the Lord.
>
> Again Jesus said, "Peace be with you! As the Father has sent me, I am sending you." And with

that he breathed on them and said, "Receive the Holy Spirit. If you forgive anyone's sins, their sins are forgiven; if you do not forgive them, they are not forgiven."

Now Thomas (also known as Didymus), one of the Twelve, was not with the disciples when Jesus came. So the other disciples told him, "We have seen the Lord!"

But he said to them, "Unless I see the nail marks in his hands and put my finger where the nails were, and put my hand into his side, I will not believe."

A week later his disciples were in the house again, and Thomas was with them. Though the doors were locked, Jesus came and stood among them and said, "Peace be with you!" Then he said to Thomas, "Put your finger here; see my hands. Reach out your hand and put it into my side. Stop doubting and believe."

Thomas said to him, "My Lord and my God!"

Then Jesus told him, "Because you have seen me, you have believed; blessed are those who have not seen and yet have believed."

Jesus performed many other signs in the presence of his disciples, which are not recorded in this book. But these are written that you may believe that Jesus is the Messiah, the Son of God, and that by believing you may have life in his name.

John 20 v 19-31

What is the explanation for the empty tomb?

Let's start with the idea that this was a myth that evolved to express spiritual truths. Perhaps it was a story that captured the idea that there is always hope. In England we tell the story of King Arthur pulling the sword *Excalibur* from the stone. It's a story that shapes English identity, but no one believes it actually happened. Are the miracle stories in the Bible like that? Are they stories that embody spiritual truths without being literally true?

People often ask, "Why do some Christians take the Bible literally?" Actually, we don't take *all* of the Bible literally. When the Bible talks about God shooting arrows of lightning, we don't think a bow appeared in the sky with giant hands firing lightning bolts. We recognise it's an image, a poetic phrase. But we do believe that what the Bible intends to affirm is true. And it clearly portrays the miracles as real events.

Consider how John tells the story of the resurrection. John was one of the people in the story. He claimed to be there. And he emphasises how he and the other apostles saw Jesus and heard Jesus and even *touched* Jesus. In the next chapter he describes the risen Jesus cooking breakfast for them (John 21 v 9-13). This is not just the continuation of an ideal. This is the continuation of a real person. John presents the resurrection as a real event. John might be lying, of course. But he's certainly not telling the story as if it is a fable. He really is claiming he saw a dead man who had been resurrected to a new life.

So let me quote David Hume again: "When anyone tells me that he saw a dead man restored to life, I immediately consider with myself whether it be more probable that this person should either deceive or be deceived or that the fact which he relates should really have happened." Hume says there are three options:

- John is deceiving people, and the resurrection story is a hoax.

- John is deceived, and the resurrection story is a mistake.

- John is right, and the resurrection story really happened.

Is John deceiving and the resurrection story a hoax?

Perhaps the resurrection was an elaborate hoax. The problem with this explanation is that it's not clear who would perpetrate such a hoax. The *opponents* of Jesus didn't *want* him to rise again, and the *followers* of Jesus didn't *expect* him to rise again. His followers certainly didn't profit from it. Far from it—many of the early leaders of the church died for their convictions while others were imprisoned.

And if the resurrection was a hoax, then the opponents of Jesus could have quickly disproved the claim by producing the body. Instead, the historical records tell us that Jesus' enemies had to pay the Roman soldiers to say that the body was stolen from under their noses (Matthew 28 v 11-15).

Is John deceived and the resurrection story a mistake?

David Hume says, "Supernatural and miraculous stories chiefly are initiated by ignorant and uncivilised people". In other words, he says, the disciples belonged to a superstitious world in which people would readily believe anything. Something happened that they couldn't explain, so they interpreted it as a resurrection.

But we mustn't judge the resurrection accounts by the standards of medieval superstition. We certainly mustn't have a kind of chronological snobbery in which we think we're superior to ancient people. They weren't gullible. Consider Thomas. He didn't believe his friends when they told him Jesus was risen (John 20 v 24-25). He demanded evidence. He needed proof. He wanted to be able to touch Jesus. He was a *sceptic*. Yet something happened that overcame his scepticism.

No one expected the resurrection. It wasn't that resurrection was a familiar concept that people would readily jump to. The Greeks and Romans didn't believe people could come back to life. When Paul went to Athens, they invited him to speak and we read, "When they heard about the resurrection of the dead, some of them sneered, but others said, 'We want to hear you again on this subject.'" (Acts 17 v 32) To the Greeks, the idea of someone rising from the dead was laughable. The Jews were divided. A Jewish group called the Sadducees rejected the idea of resurrection altogether. Other Jews did believe in the resurrection, but only at the end of time. What none of them were expecting was for someone to rise from the dead in the middle of history.

Without exception, when the risen Jesus appeared to people, they were shocked and surprised. They mistook him for someone else or thought he was a ghost (John 20 v 15; Luke 24 v 37). No one expected Jesus to rise from the dead. They weren't all waiting to jump to that conclusion without any basis in truth.

Is John right and the resurrection story really happened?

David Hume says, "No testimony is sufficient to establish a miracle, unless the testimony be of such a kind that its falsehood would be more miraculous than the fact which it endeavours to establish". In other words, which is more unlikely—that the disciples were wrong or the disciples were right? That the disciples gave their lives for a story they'd made up or that an all-powerful Creator God was able to raise his Son from the dead? I suggest that the resurrection of Jesus is the best explanation of the empty tomb.

I realise my arguments are not decisive in and of themselves. There's no QED moment in the argument. But if God exists, then he must surely have the capacity to perform miracles. That can't be proved scientifically, but neither can it be *disproved* scientifically. Science looks at regular causes and effects. But miracles are *by definition* interruptions of normal cause and effect. So by definition they're outside the scope of science. This is not a debate between science and religion. It's a debate between atheism and theism in which plenty of eminent scientists line up on both sides of the debate.

The real issue is not reason, but love

Here's where Hume and I agree: Hume argues that *desire* rather than reason is what drives human thought and behaviour. He says, "Reason is, and ought only to be, the slave of the passions, and can never pretend to any other office than to serve and obey them".[7] Or consider this quote from Richard Lewontin, the Professor of Genetics at Harvard University:

> *Our willingness to accept scientific claims that are against common sense is the key to an understanding of the real struggle between science and the supernatural. We take the side of science **in spite** of the patent absurdity of some of its constructs … because we have a prior commitment, a commitment to materialism. It is not that the methods and institutions of science somehow compel us to accept a material explanation of the phenomenal world, but, on the contrary, that we are forced by our **a priori** adherence to material causes to create an apparatus of investigation and a set of concepts that produce material explanations, no matter how counter-intuitive, no matter how mystifying to the uninitiated. Moreover, that materialism is absolute, for we cannot allow a Divine Foot in the door.[8]*

In other words, Lewontin rejects miracles because he doesn't want God. It's an admission of prejudice. I don't say that to be rude or dismissive. We all have

7   David Hume, *A Treatise on Human Nature* (1739-1740), ed. L. A. Selby-Bigge (1888), Book 2, Part 3, Section 3, p 415.

8   Richard Lewontin, "Billions and Billions of Demons", *The New York Review*, 9 January 1997, p 31 (a review of *The Demon-Haunted World: Science as a Candle in the Dark* by Carl Sagan, 1997), http://www.nybooks.com/articles/1297.

our prejudices. Christians are also prejudiced. We're inclined to believe the Bible's miracles because we *do* want God.

The point is this:

- If you know God and love God, then you won't have a problem believing miracles.

- If you hate the idea of God, then you'll readily find reasons to reject both his existence and his miracles.

The real issue is not reason. The real issue is *desire* or *love*.

I can't definitively prove to you that the miracles in the Bible happened. In fact, even if someone performed a miracle in front of your eyes, that wouldn't be enough. There were plenty of people who saw the miracles of Jesus—and then plotted to kill him, as we shall see. If you're determined to reject God, then you'll always find reasons to reject his miracles. But I do want people to recognise that believing in miracles is rational if God exists. You may still reject God, but you'll be doing so for other reasons—reasons that have more to do with what you love than what you think.

Why did Jesus tell people not to tell others about his miracles?

Throughout Mark's Gospel Jesus tells spirits and people not to talk about him, especially after he has done a miracle (Mark 1 v 25, 34, 44; 3 v 12; 5 v 43; 7 v 36; 8 v 26, 30; 9 v 9). The reason for this becomes clear as the Gospel unfolds.

Jesus is God's King. But he is not the kind of king that people expect. He is the King who will die for his people. So he doesn't want people proclaiming his power until they have realised he is the King who must die. He doesn't want people following him simply because they are interested in what they can get from him—whether that is political power or a quick cure. He wants people who recognise the guilt of their sin and recognise the pardon of the cross.

Chapter 2

Do miracles happen today?

In the early eighteenth century a number of miracles were reported at the grave of Abbé François de Pâris in France. Abbé Pâris was a deacon in the Catholic church whose simple, self-disciplined lifestyle attracted devotees. But François was associated with Jansenism, a movement which was opposed by the Catholic hierarchy, and so to the authorities these miracles were a problem. As a result, the King of France ordered a sign to be placed at his grave, "By command of the king, God is forbidden to work any more miracles here".

Is God forbidden to work miracles here?

Before we decide whether miracles happen today, we had better be clear what we're talking about. What is a miracle?

It turns out that defining a miracle is not as straightforward as you might first imagine.

An extraordinary act of God?

You might say, "A miracle is an extraordinary act". According to this definition, a miracle is something we don't normally expect—something out of the ordinary. It's not normal for people to walk on water. So when Jesus walks on water, it's a miracle.

The problem with this definition is that it's hard to define what's "normal" and people differ in what they "expect". In 2016 Leicester City Football Club won the Premier League—the top soccer competition in England. Over the previous twenty years only four clubs had won the league—four big clubs with deep pockets. Leicester couldn't match the financial resources of the big clubs so, even though Leicester topped the league throughout much of the season, everyone assumed they would falter. But they didn't falter and went on to win. It was out of the ordinary. The previous season Leicester had only just escaped relegation and at the beginning of the new season bookmakers had offered odds of 5,000 to 1 on them winning the league. No one expected it to happen. It was an extraordinary accomplishment. Was it a miracle? Certainly people used that language rhetorically. But intuitively I suspect most of us, even if we are Leicester supporters, would not regard it as a divine miracle.

A supernatural act of God?

You might say, "A miracle is a supernatural act or an act of God". Making a cup of tea is not a miracle because it's the result of my actions—pouring boiling water into a teapot containing a tea bag. There's no need for God to intervene in the making of my cup of tea. But walking on water is another matter. Walking on water is a miracle because it's a divine act. Human beings don't have the capacity to walk on water (at least not without cheating, as magicians do when they use hidden Perspex platforms).

The problem with this definition is that it assumes God is involved in some activities (miracles), but not involved in other activities (everything else). But God is involved in *everything* that happens. In this sense, everything is an act of God.

Let's suppose I pray for rain tomorrow. Perhaps God will answer my prayer by sending water out of a blue sky. Or perhaps he will arrange for clouds to form through the regular operation of the water cycle. God is involved in both these scenarios—rain from blue skies and rain from clouds. Both are acts of God. Are both miracles? If we define miracles as acts of God, then everything is a miracle.

In the Bible, some events that we think of as miracles—and which are called miracles in the Bible itself— can be explained by natural causes—albeit on an unusual scale or with perfect timing. During the time of the Prophet Elijah there were three years of drought which ended with heavy rain. Nothing unusual about that. Both drought and rain are common enough natural phenomena. Except that the drought came exactly when God said it would. It will come, said God, "at my word" (1 Kings 17 v 1). Predicting a dry day is good meteorology; predicting three years of drought is divine prophecy. The rains, too, came exactly when

Elijah predicted they would and as a direct response to his prayers (1 Kings 18 v 41-46; James 5 v 17-18).

A direct act of God?

You might say, "A miracle is an immediate or direct act of God". I'm using the word "immediate" here in the sense of "without mediation" or "without means". Miracles, according to this definition, represent God's "direct" intervention into the world. Clearly some acts involve God's unmediated intervention. Think of the virgin birth. The conception of Jesus took place without any mediating factors. God didn't work through a man to make Mary pregnant. Neither did he use the equivalent of IVF. It was a direct act of God.

The problem with this definition, however, is that other acts—acts described in the Bible as miracles—involve God using means.

Consider the parting of the Red Sea in Exodus 14. The King of Egypt has let the people of Israel go, but has then changed his mind. So God's people find themselves caught between the advancing Egyptian army and the Red Sea. But then God parts the waters of the sea, so his people can walk through on dry ground. When the Egyptian army tries to follow, the waters fall back and the Egyptians are drowned. Reflecting on what has happened, Moses sings:

Who among the gods
  is like you, LORD?
Who is like you –
  majestic in holiness,

awesome in glory,
    working wonders?   *Exodus 15 v 11*

"Wonders" is one of the Bible's words for what we call miracles. By any standard this is a remarkable miracle. Indeed, the Psalmist uses the word "miracles" in Psalm 77 v 11 to describe events that include the parting of the Red Sea (v 19). Yet consider how the Bible describes what happens:

Moses stretched out his hand over the sea, and all that night the LORD drove the sea back with a strong east wind and turned it into dry land. The waters were divided, and the Israelites went through the sea on dry ground, with a wall of water on their right and on their left.
                                          Exodus 14 v 21-22

The waters parted because a strong east wind separated them. In other words, this was a natural phenomenon. Yes, it was on an unprecedented scale. Yes, the timing was just right. Yet there is a natural explanation. One cause and effect is Moses stretching out his hand at God's command and the resulting escape for God's people—this is a divine miracle that only the Lord could accomplish. Another cause and effect is the wind and the resulting dry ground—this is an act of nature. It was a miracle, but God used natural means to accomplish it.

How the Bible defines miracles

When we examine how the Bible defines miracles, we find it is more interested in the *purpose* of miracles. Miracles are "extraordinary" and they are "acts of God". But this is not sufficient. They are also used by God to rescue his people or reveal his glory.

When God calls Moses to lead his people out of slavery in Egypt, he tells Moses:

> But I know that the king of Egypt will not let you go unless a mighty hand compels him. So I will stretch out my hand and strike the Egyptians with all the wonders that I will perform among them. After that, he will let you go.　*Exodus 3 v 19-20*

Why does God perform "wonders"? To compel Pharaoh to let God's people go free.

God also sends Moses to the people with an arsenal of "signs": a hand that turns leprous, a staff that turns into a snake, a river that turns to blood.

> "This," said the Lord, "is so that they may believe that the Lord, the God of their fathers—the God of Abraham, the God of Isaac and the God of Jacob—has appeared to you."　*Exodus 4 v 1-9*

Why does God perform "signs"? To convince his people that the Lord their God is rescuing them. But God is not just revealing himself to Israel. God says he will do "mighty acts of judgment" so that "the Egyptians will know that I am the Lord" and "that my name might be proclaimed in all the earth" (Exodus 7 v 4-5; 9 v 16).

We find the same pattern in the New Testament. Having described how Jesus turned water into wine, the Apostle John comments, "What Jesus did here in Cana of Galilee was the first of the signs through which he revealed his glory; and his disciples believed in him" (John 2 v 11). Indeed, again and again in his Gospel, John pairs a miracle with an extended explanation of who Jesus is. Jesus, for example, feeds 5,000 men plus women and children with just five loaves and two fish, and then he explains that he himself is "the bread of life" (John 6 v 35). The miracle is a sign of the salvation Jesus brings.

The Bible uses three words to describe what we call miracles.[9] We've met them already.

- "sign"—an event that points to something else

- "wonder"—an event that evokes amazement

- "miracle" or "mighty work"—an act of unusual power

Sometimes all three terms are used together:

- "Fellow Israelites, listen to this: Jesus of Nazareth was a man accredited by God to you by miracles, wonders and signs, which God did among you through him, as you yourselves know" (Acts 2 v 22).

- "I persevered in demonstrating among you the marks of a true apostle, including signs, wonders and miracles" (2 Corinthians 12 v 12).

---

9   Donald Macleod, *Behold Your God* (Christian Focus, 1995), p 78.

- "God also testified to it by signs, wonders and various miracles, and by gifts of the Holy Spirit distributed according to his will" (Hebrews 2 v 4).

Combining the meaning of these terms, we can define miracles as *amazing acts of power through which God reveals his glory and rescues his people.*

Understanding miracles in this way explains why in the Bible people often react to them in surprising ways, even negative ways. On one occasion, the disciples of Jesus had been fishing all night without success. Jesus urges them to try one more time, which they do against their instincts. This time they catch an amazing haul of fish. What's Peter's reaction? "When Simon Peter saw this, he fell at Jesus' knees and said, 'Go away from me, Lord; I am a sinful man!'" (Luke 5 v 8). You might imagine that Peter would be excited to have witnessed such an extraordinary phenomenon. Or that he would be mentally counting the money he could earn from selling the massive catch. But, no, he falls down in fear. This miracle is a revelation of God's glory in Christ. And, faced with the presence of God, Peter is filled with fear and convicted of sin.

On another occasion Jesus healed a man who had been possessed by a legion of demons. The possessed man must have been a terrifying prospect. People had repeatedly tried to restrain him, but he had always torn the chains apart. Yet when the people of the town see the man liberated from his demons, they are even more afraid. "When they came to Jesus, they saw the man who had been possessed by the legion of demons, sitting there, dressed and in his right mind; and they were afraid" (Mark 5 v 15). An uncontrollable man is frightening; the God-man who can control an uncontrollable man is even more frightening.

The fuzzy world of miracles

The point of this exercise is not simply to play word games or to mess with your head. There's a serious point which is revealed in the difficulty of defining miracles: God is much more involved in our world than a focus on what we call miracles might assume.

Our definitions of miracles inevitably end up being a bit fuzzy because God is actively involved in both the extraordinary and ordinary. He's involved in supernatural events and natural events. He's involved immediately and intermediately—he intervenes in our world directly and he intervenes indirectly through other means. He answers prayer through supernatural interventions and through natural causes.

Psalm 136 praises God because "his loves endures for ever" and the Psalmist urges us to give thanks "to him who alone does great wonders" (v 1-4). Those "wonders" include the creation of the earth and stars (v 5-9), the miracles that took place during the exodus from Egypt (v 10-16), and the defeat of great kings during the conquest of Canaan (v 17-24). But the psalm ends with this wonder, "He gives food to every creature" (v 25). God's day-by-day care of his creation is a miracle.

Miracles in the medieval and modern world

The medieval world was a world full of wonders. Almost everything was seen as a direct intervention from outside. Often events were attributed to God. But they could also be attributed to angels, saints, devils, relics and even fairies. People routinely assumed that there were supernatural causes behind daily events. They looked for spiritual explanations of what happened in their lives. An illness or a crop failure might be seen as an act of divine judgment or the curse of a witch. The boundary between the spiritual and physical world was porous.

Then, with the growth of modern science, we began to find explanations in nature for a host of phenomena. The water cycle explained the weather. Bacteria and viruses explained the spread of illnesses. Christians began to distinguish between natural causes and miraculous causes.

The problem was that secular thinkers reframed this distinction as a distinction between what could be explained by science and what could not (yet) be explained by science. As a result, the more science advanced in its understanding of the world, the less room there was for God. The miraculous was edged out of the world. The world became "disenchanted".

God was removed from the picture. The Canadian philosopher, Charles Taylor, talks about "the immanent frame". The modern world thinks of the world as a picture in a frame. The world around us—what we can see, hear, touch, taste and smell—lies within the frame of the picture. And the frame is a kind of boundary. If there is anything outside the picture (like God), then it doesn't enter. Everything is immanent (existing or operating within the frame); there's no transcendent reality operating within the frame from outside.

Perhaps somewhat surprisingly, Taylor argues that people who want to make much of miracles are actually buying into this modern worldview. Why? Because they assume God is normally absent from the world, but they think God occasionally turns up to do something spectacular. Maybe they hope God might intervene on a monthly or weekly basis, but at other times he's not involved. God becomes an occasional-Lord rather than an always-Lord. This way of thinking would have been unrecognisable in the medieval world. To the medieval mind everything was caused by God or Satan.

We can't return to the medieval world because we now know too much about natural causes. We know the reason that lightning strikes is electrostatic discharges (or at least we can readily look that up on Wikipedia). We don't assume that lightning bolts have come straight from heaven or hell. But Christians can't be pure modernists either, as if modern science has closed the door to divine involvement in the world.

The story of the move from a medieval to a modern worldview in Western culture highlights two dangers facing Christians today:

- The danger of seeing the world as if it is closed to God

- The danger of seeing miracles as God's normal way of working

The danger of seeing the world as if it is closed to God

We live in a deeply secular culture which views the world as being closed to God. It lives within Taylor's "immanent frame". Our culture largely assumes that this world and natural causes are all there is. Therefore miracles don't happen.

Christians can do a version of this. We vehemently defend the miracles that took place during the ministry of Jesus. But we can be sceptical about miracles today. We can be shaped by the rationalism of our age. We want to appear credible to our unbelieving friends.

As a result, we can become "functional deists". A deist is someone who believes in God and perhaps believes God was involved in the creation of the world, but who also believes God is no longer active in his world. The god of the deists is distant and detached. Christians today can believe God made the world and sent his Son to redeem the world. We can pray for God to act. But in practice we often don't really expect him to get involved.

Or we become "functional dualists". A common feature of the modern world is a sharp distinction between mind and matter. And Christians sometimes apply this distinction to God's involvement in the world. We restrict God's action to inner spiritual change. We pray for unbelievers to be converted and for Christians to grow in godliness. We're happy with the idea that God impacts "minds" or "souls". But we're much more hesitant to pray for "matter" to change—for bodies to heal or engines to start or weather to improve.

But this world is not closed to God. Modern humanity may have erected the barricades to keep God out. But actually there's nothing new in that. The Psalmist describes how the kings of the world have always risen up to reject God's reign (Psalm 2 v 1-3). God's response? "The One enthroned in heaven laughs; the LORD scoffs at them" (Psalm 2 v 4). God still rules in heaven and he still intervenes on earth. "[God] is not confronted with some unalterable causal nexus or a closed system of natural laws, but with a universe which is utterly open to him, pervaded by him and totally plastic in his hands".[10]

The danger of seeing miracles as God's normal way of working

A second danger is to be always looking for miracles as if they represent God's normal way of working. People who constantly look for miracles can appear to have a high belief in God's involvement in the world. But actually this approach reflects a low level of expectation of God's involvement. Essentially, as Taylor argues, it buys into the closed world of modernity. It assumes that most things happen apart from God, but hopes for a few exceptions every now and then.

When Noah finally stepped from the ark after the flood, he built an altar and offered a sacrifice to God. In response the LORD declared:

As long as the earth endures,
seedtime and harvest,

---

10 Donald Macleod, *Behold Your God* (Christian Focus, 1995), p 78.

cold and heat,
summer and winter,
day and night
will never cease.   *Genesis 8 v 22*

The world is not a chaotic series of random events.
When you plant a seed, it normally grows to produce a
harvest. Winter normally follows summer; day follows
night. If you throw a ball into the air, it normally falls to
the ground. If you put your hand into a fire, it normally
gets burned. God is not bound by these patterns—they
normally happen, but there are exceptions. God is free
to act in abnormal ways. But he has given these patterns
as a gift. They allow us to plan, to plant, to predict, to
act responsibly.

For forty years, while the people of Israel wandered in
the wilderness, God sent manna from heaven each day
to meet their daily needs. But shortly after they entered
the promised land, we read:

On the evening of the fourteenth day of the
month, while camped at Gilgal on the plains of
Jericho, the Israelites celebrated the Passover. The
day after the Passover, that very day, they ate some
of the produce of the land: unleavened bread and
roasted grain. The manna stopped the day after
they ate this food from the land; there was no
longer any manna for the Israelites, but that year
they ate the produce of Canaan.   *Joshua 5 v 10-12*

As soon as they ate the produce of the land, the manna stopped. Is this because God's power ran out or because he stopped caring? No. It's because the people could now feed themselves through natural means.

What we think of as miracles are, by definition, exceptional. They are not the norm, and we have no right to expect them as the norm. Theologian John Frame says miracles are possible, but not probable. If they were probable, then they would not be miracles since miracles are by definition extraordinary acts that amaze us.[11]

The importance of seeing God as constantly at work in his world

Those who assume that the world is closed to God have a small view of God. But those who see miracles as frequent also have a small view of God. God is much more active in our world. *Everything* is an act of God. Sometimes God works directly and sometimes he works through secondary causes; sometimes he works through what we call miracles and sometimes he works through natural means. But God is always at work. Not every act of God, says John Stott, is a miracle. "He normally works according to the natural order which he has himself established. At the same time, he is not imprisoned by nature or the laws of nature."[12]

We need a big view of God's providence. Everything is caused by God, including those things for which we can also identify a natural cause.

---

11 John Frame, *The Doctrine of God* (P&R, 2012), p 276.

12 John Stott, *"But I Say to You": Christ the Controversialist* (IVP UK, 2013), p 56.

- If someone is cured in a way that defies scientific explanations, then God is at work and we should praise him.

- If someone is cured through the work of doctors using routine medical procedures, then God is at work and we should praise him.

- If someone is not healed, then God is at work and we should praise him.

God's purposes can be fulfilled through miracles. But God's purposes can also be fulfilled through natural causes. We have an always-Lord; not an occasional-Lord.

The pastoral pay-off of this view of God is significant.

First, it means God is involved in our lives all the time. In every moment of every day, God is actively involved in blessing you. He is giving you gifts—life, breath, food, sunshine, health, family, beauty, laughter. On and on the list goes.

> Let them give thanks to the LORD for his
> unfailing love
>   and his wonderful deeds for mankind,
> for he satisfies the thirsty
>   and fills the hungry with good things.
>
> *Psalm 107 v 8-9*

Second, the bad things that happen in our lives are also gifts from God. They are not a sign that God has failed or that we have failed. Suppose you're ill and pray for a miracle, but no miracle comes. Is the problem that God is absent or powerless? That's the assumption of secularism. Or is the problem your lack of faith? That's the assumption of many who expect miracles as a norm. But what if the reason is that God has a bigger purpose in mind? What if God is using your problem to make you more like his Son—just as he promises he will?

> And we know that in all things God works for the good of those who love him, who have been called according to his purpose. For those God foreknew he also predestined to be conformed to the image of his Son, that he might be the firstborn among many brothers and sisters. *Romans 8 v 28-29*

God is involved in our lives all the time. So we thank him for his blessings and ask him to help us trust him when things are hard. And in everything we ask him to make us more like his Son.

How should I respond when I hear a claim that a miracle has happened?

Many of us tend to one extreme or the other when we hear a claim of a miracle. Either we respond with excitement, wanting to know more and wishing we had seen it for ourselves—or we dismiss the claim as an unlikely boast, or file it away with other urban myths.

We have seen that God can still perform miracles today, but that this isn't his usual way of working. For that reason, it's wise to be cautious when someone claims that a miracle has happened. At the same time, let's be careful not to dismiss the possibility of a miracle. God is still a God of both power and compassion.

We especially need to tread carefully when the story comes from a different group or denomination. It's all too easy for our scepticism actually to be a form of envy. When Jesus' followers tried to stop a man who wasn't a disciple from performing miracles, Jesus' response to them was, "Do not stop him ... for whoever is not against you is for you" (Luke 9 v 50).

One helpful approach is to ask where the glory for any miracle is given. Since we know that miracles point to the truth about Jesus, we should question anything that gives glory to people or distracts from the glory of Christ crucified.

Chapter 3

Why are there fewer miracles today?

In his book exploring the growth of evangelical Christianity, *The Hallelujah Revolution*,[13] the journalist Ian Cotton describes how Lloyd Kuehl, an American Christian, travelled from the United States to join a group of British Christians praying for the healing of a man called John who was suffering from liver cancer. As it turned out, Lloyd arrived to find that John had already died. But Lloyd felt that God said to him, "I will raise him from the dead". Fired by this conviction, the group continued to pray that John would be brought to life. Four days later they gave up and John was cremated.

In the previous chapter we saw that no one has switched God off. Modern humanity has not closed the doors of the world, leaving God on the outside, unable to get in.

So can we expect miracles to happen in the way they did during the ministry of Jesus and the apostles?

---

13 Ian Cotton, *The Hallelujah Revolution: The Rise of the New Christians* (Little, Brown, 1995).

Should our expectation of miracles be shaped by what we read in the Gospels and the book of Acts?

Some people think so. We live in the age of the Spirit, they argue, and so we should expect the story of Acts to continue in our own lives with a miracle for every chapter of our lives.

Yet it's hard to avoid a recognition that miracles don't happen today in the way they did in the time of Jesus. They don't happen with the same frequency and they don't happen on the same scale. Occasionally stories circulate of people being raised from the dead, though they're usually a few steps removed from the person telling you the story. No one today walks on water. No one stills storms—at least not in the instantaneous way that Jesus did.

It's striking how most miracles today involve internal illnesses like cancer. I've known people whose tumours have disappeared, with non-Christian doctors using the word "miracle" to describe what has happened. Yet I've never met anyone whose amputated limb has grown back. I'm not being cynical about cured cancers. I've seen dramatic answers to prayer in my own church. But I've not seen anything that matches the scale and scope of New Testament miracles.

How do we make sense of this gap between then and now? Some of those who believe that apostolic-style miracles continue today do so by promising that a new age of miracles will dawn some time soon. Others argue that we don't see more miracles because of our lack of expectation—if we had more faith, then we would see more miracles.

Perhaps there is something in these arguments. But there are other reasons to suppose God performed more miracles in the past than he does now. We need to consider again the purpose of miracles. The Bible shows us that:

- Miracles confirm that Jesus is the Saviour of the world.

- Miracles confirm that Jesus is stronger than Satan.

- Miracles confirm that the Bible is the word of God.

Miracles confirm that Jesus is the Saviour of the world

On the day of Pentecost, Peter told the crowd, "Jesus of Nazareth was a man accredited by God to you by miracles, wonders and signs, which God did among you through him, as you yourselves know" (Acts 2 v 22). The miracles that Jesus performed were intended to accredit him as God's promised Saviour-King. They reveal and confirm his identity. John says:

> Jesus performed many other signs in the presence of his disciples, which are not recorded in this book. But these are written that you may believe that Jesus is the Messiah, the Son of God, and that by believing you may have life in his name.
>
> *John 20 v 30-31*

The miracles of Jesus are unique because Jesus was unique. The miracles of Jesus were the signs that he is the Son of God sent by God as the Saviour of the world. Jesus himself said:

> Do not believe me unless I do the works of my Father. But if I do them, even though you do not believe me, believe the works, that you may know and understand that the Father is in me, and I in the Father.
> *John 10 v 37-38*

I don't do miracles like Jesus because I'm not the Son of God. Today people don't normally walk on water. Thousands of people are not normally fed from five loaves. Not normally. Things like that don't happen in our world. But that's the point. Miracles aren't normal.

Miracles point to the salvation that is found in Jesus. Our world is a world of hunger, pain, suffering and want. Even in the West, where most people have enough to eat, we still live in want. We're still unsatisfied. We may not long for bread, but we long for meaning, intimacy, justice, fulfilment, community, purpose and joy. We long for the world to be sorted out.

That's why we find Jesus' miracles hard to believe. They don't "fit" in this broken world. But that's not because what he did couldn't happen or didn't happen. To judge his miracles by our experience of what happens in this world is to miss the point. His miracles don't belong in this world because they're a glimpse of *another* world. They're the start of a new world; signs of God's coming world.

In Luke's account of the life of Jesus, Jesus heals a woman who has been haemorrhaging blood for twelve years. Jesus says to her, "Daughter, your faith has healed you. Go in peace" (Luke 8 v 48). The phrase is literally "your faith has *saved* you". Luke was a doctor. He had plenty of medical words in his vocabulary. He uses a different one in the previous verse when he says the woman was "instantly healed". But here in verse 48 he uses the word "saved". This healing is a picture of salvation.

We find the same pattern in Acts 4 where Peter and John are put on trial for healing a lame man. Peter declares:

> If we are being called to account today for an act of kindness shown to a man who was lame and are being asked how he was healed, then know this, you and all the people of Israel: it is by the name of Jesus Christ of Nazareth.　　　　*Acts 4 v 9-10*

Again the word "healed" is literally "saved". Peter uses the same word moments later when he says, "Salvation is found in no one else, for there is no other name under heaven given to mankind by which we must be saved" (Acts 4 v 12).

The miracles of Jesus are a sign that he is the Saviour, and they are a picture of his salvation. The very language of "sign" is significant. Think of a signpost. It points beyond itself, and it would be foolish to confuse the sign with the reality. If you saw a sign to a beauty spot, you would follow the sign to find the ultimate destination rather than setting out your picnic around the signpost. The miracles of Jesus point beyond themselves to the coming new world that Jesus brings.

The miracles of Jesus and of the first apostles are a glimpse of the renewal of all things in the new creation. They show us what God's salvation is like. They show us who Jesus is. The reason that they feel strange to us is because they don't belong in our broken world. They are the promise and beginning of a new world.

Our world—the world humanity has created—is a world of famine, injustice, division and hurt. But the kingdom of Jesus is very different. For a moment in history we were given a glimpse of that coming reality. The poor were fed. The sick were healed. The dead were raised. Evil was defeated. This is God's future. And it can be your future if you put your faith in Jesus. We don't need miracles in the same way today because we have the resurrection. The resurrection is the ultimate promise and sign of God's new world.

Miracles confirm that Jesus is stronger than Satan

There were many occasions during the ministry of Jesus when he cast a demon out of a person. Here's an example from Mark 1:

> They went to Capernaum, and when the Sabbath came, Jesus went into the synagogue and began to teach. The people were amazed at his teaching, because he taught them as one who had authority, not as the teachers of the law. Just then a man in their synagogue who was possessed by an impure spirit cried out, "What do you want with us, Jesus of Nazareth? Have you come to destroy us? I know who you are—the Holy One of God!"

"Be quiet!" said Jesus sternly. "Come out of him!" The impure spirit shook the man violently and came out of him with a shriek.

The people were all so amazed that they asked each other, "What is this? A new teaching—and with authority! He even gives orders to impure spirits and they obey him."   *Mark 1 v 21-27*

A few verses later, Mark tells us that Jesus "drove out many demons" (Mark 1 v 34). Mark also tells us that, "Whenever the impure spirits saw him, they fell down before him and cried out, 'You are the Son of God'" (Mark 3 v 11). Moreover, Jesus gave authority to his disciples "to drive out demons" (Mark 3 v 15). On one occasion Jesus released a man from a legion of demons with just a word (Mark 5 v 6-13).

Why do we not see this sort of thing today? Or at least why do we not see it on the same scale? Some people regard all sorts of problems as caused by demons and requiring some kind of exorcism. Are they right?

Some people suggest demon-possession was just the way people in the first century mistakenly understood mental illness. But this does not account for the conversations Jesus had with the demons possessing people—like the demon in the story from Mark 1 above. Jesus clearly saw what was happening as a confrontation between himself and the devil. At one point Matthew describes the impact of Jesus in Syria, "News about him spread all over Syria, and people brought to him all who were ill with various diseases, those suffering severe pain, the demon-possessed, those having seizures, and the paralysed; and he healed them" (Matthew 4 v 24). Notice the way that Matthew distinguishes between demon-possession and seizures, since these are separate items in his list of the issues Jesus resolves. It seems that Matthew, at least, was not confusing epilepsy with demonic possession.

To understand why demon possession is less frequent today, we need to recognise what was distinctive back then in the ministry of Jesus and what is distinctive about the work of Satan in our generation.

First, what was distinctive about the ministry of Jesus?

1. Satan was intent on disrupting the work of Jesus

It's hardly surprising that we should see Satan being particularly active during the ministry of Jesus. The Son of God had come to earth to rescue God's people and so Satan focused all his efforts on thwarting that mission. It may even be that the demons were attempting to counterfeit the incarnation. At the incarnation the Son of God became human so that Jesus was truly God and truly man. It may be that Satan did his best to copy this by sending his demons to possess people. These could not be a true incarnation, of course, because a demon is neither truly God, nor can it become truly human. But it can control a human body.

2. Jesus was intent on destroying the work of Satan

"The reason the Son of God appeared," says 1 John 3 v 8, "was to destroy the devil's work." Ultimately Jesus would defeat Satan at the cross (Colossians 2 v 15). But every exorcism was a sign of what he had come to do.

This is how Jesus explains his exorcisms in Mark 3. After the sequence of stories from Mark's Gospel listed above, in which Jesus casts out demons, the religious leaders offer their own explanation of what is happening. "By the prince of demons he is driving out demons," they say (Mark 3 v 22). That makes no sense, replies Jesus, because then Satan would defeat himself.

Then Jesus continues, "In fact, no one can enter a strong man's house without first tying him up. Then he can plunder the strong man's house" (Mark 3 v 27). The strong man in this word-picture is Satan. Satan holds people in his grip. But Jesus has come as one who is stronger than the strong man. It is striking that shortly afterwards in Mark's Gospel Jesus literally meets a strong man whom no one can bind, a man possessed by a demon. People have repeatedly tried to restrain him, but each time "he tore the chains apart and broke the irons on his feet" (Mark 5 v 4). But Jesus expels the demons within him and restores the man to his right mind. This man simultaneously pictures Satan—the strong man, who is overcome by Jesus—and at the same time he represents those under Satan's power whom Jesus releases and restores.

Every exorcism is a sign that Jesus is about to bind Satan's power and release people from his power. This is what happened at the cross. Satan's claim over us was broken as Jesus bore the penalty of sin in our place. As a result, we are set free. We are the plunder Jesus claims.

Having seen what's distinctive about the ministry of Jesus, we also need to recognise what is distinctive about the ministry of Satan in our generation. Taking possession of someone is not Satan's only way of working, and it's not his main way of working. He is "the father of lies". "When he lies," says Jesus, "he speaks his native language, for he is a liar and the father of lies" (John 8 v 44). It was through lying that Satan did his first and worst work, persuading humanity to rebel against God in the Garden of Eden. Satan has many ways of working, but today it would seem that his principle way of working is through the lie of materialism—materialism as a philosophy and materialism as a lifestyle.

a) Materialism as a philosophy

Materialism is the view that the material world—the stuff we can see, feel, taste—is all there is. It denies that there is a spiritual, heavenly or transcendent world with an eternal future. Today, at least in the West, Satan is busy at work persuading people that this world is all there is. That means, of course, that most people think there is no Satan (since he is a spiritual being). But presumably that does not bother him too much, because it also means that people think there is no God (or no God who intervenes in the world). This means secular people are less likely to be directly involved in occult activity and so less likely to come under the direct influence of Satan. But a culture in which Satan was openly active would alert people to a supernatural realm and therefore also to God.

b) Materialism as a lifestyle

Materialism can also be a lifestyle. This is the way of life that makes material possessions and physical pleasures the priority. People may or may not believe in God, but what matters to them is what they can earn, buy, own, eat and have. Today Satan blinds people by distracting them with the pursuit of possessions and pleasures.

Imagine a boy standing in front of an advertisement for a funfair. Little Jack is completely mesmerised by its bold colours and glowing promises. His parents are trying to pull him away so they can head off to the funfair together. But Jack refuses to move his feet or lift his eyes from the poster. He refuses the bigger joys of the funfair because he can't see beyond what is front of him. In the same way, the good things of this world—food, sex, pleasure—are all designed to point us to the Giver, the beautiful, generous God who invites us to share his joy. But today Satan transfixes us with the pleasures of this world so we never look up to see the glory of God.

When Jesus liberated the demon-possessed man in the Capernaum synagogue, what the people remarked on was the authority of his words: "What words these are! With authority and power he gives orders to impure spirits and they come out!" (Luke 4 v 36). And today the main way we confront the work of Satan is to proclaim the word of God. We counter the Satanic lie of materialism with the truth of Scripture.

Miracles confirm that the Bible is the word of God

Miracles are not uniform throughout the Bible story. They're clustered around key moments: Moses, Elijah and Elisha, and Jesus and the apostles. Centuries went by without any miracle being recorded—from Noah to

Abraham, from Abraham to Moses, from Malachi to Jesus. Even Moses spent 80 years without seeing a miracle.

Moreover, miracles are clustered at the beginning of the book of Acts. The amazing miracles listed in Acts 5 v 12-16 are described as events belonging to the past with no suggestion that they're still normal for Luke's readers. In Acts 19 v 11-12 Luke says, "God did extraordinary miracles through Paul, so that even handkerchiefs and aprons that had touched him were taken to those who were ill, and their illnesses were cured and the evil spirits left them". Again, the word "extraordinary" suggests they are no longer the ordinary experience of Luke's readers. Even in the apostolic period, it seems, miracles were becoming rarer as time went on. They don't feature in the later books of the New Testament.

Why are there these clusters of miracles? It's because miracles confirm God's revelation. They accredit God's word. "Miracles are not evenly spread throughout Scripture, but appear in clusters," says John Stott, because "their clear purpose was to authenticate a fresh stage of God's self-disclosure to his chosen people".[14]

Consider those three main clusters: (1) Moses; (2) Elijah and Elisha; and (3) Jesus and the apostles.

Moses was the one through whom God gave the Law. Not only did he lead Israel out of slavery in Egypt, he also brought them to Mount Sinai and went up to the mountain to receive the covenant. The miracles associ-

---

14 John Stott, "But I Say to You": Christ the Controversialist (IVP UK, 2013), p 56.

ated with Moses all combine to confirm the revelation of God in the Law, the first five books of the Bible.

The ministries of Elijah and Elisha dominate the history of Israel as a nation in the promised land. They were the archetypal prophets and as such they present the revelation of God in prophecy. So the miracles associated with Elijah and Elisha confirm the revelation of God in prophecy.

This is the main reason why it's Moses and Elijah who appear alongside Jesus on the mountain when Jesus is transfigured (Mark 9 v 4). They come to represent the old covenant. Their presence is God's way of saying that Jesus is the fulfilment of the Old Testament. The Old Testament is confirmed as the word of God pointing to God's revelation in his Son; and Jesus is confirmed as the fulfilment of the promises of the Old Testament.

So it is that the Father's voice from heaven does not say, "Gaze on him" (even though Jesus is transfigured into dazzling white glory). Instead the Father says, "Listen to him" (Mark 9 v 7). All the miracles performed by Moses, Elijah, Elisha and Jesus are there to back up this command: "Listen to him". Pay attention to the word of God in the Old and New Testaments.

What about the apostles? Jesus is the ultimate revelation. His words, works and life all reveal God. He is the perfect image of God for he himself is God. He is the greatest Prophet, the Word made flesh. So if God's revelation reaches its climax in Jesus, why do miracles continue in the ministries of the apostles?

The issue is this: you and I weren't there to see the miracles of Jesus or hear his words. God's ultimate revelation in Jesus is all well and good. But how can we access it? Are we left with rumours and hearsay? Must we juggle competing versions of Jesus?

No. For God has made provision for his revelation in Christ to be permanently and accurately recorded. This is where the apostles come in. In the night before his death Jesus told his first disciples:

> All this I have spoken while still with you. But the Advocate, the Holy Spirit, whom the Father will send in my name, will teach you all things and will remind you of everything I have said to you.
>
> *John 14 v 25-26*

> I have much more to say to you, more than you can now bear. But when he, the Spirit of truth, comes, he will guide you into all the truth. He will not speak on his own; he will speak only what he hears, and he will tell you what is yet to come. He will glorify me because it is from me that he will receive what he will make known to you. All that belongs to the Father is mine. That is why I said the Spirit will receive from me what he will make known to you.
>
> *John 16 v 12-15*

This is not a promise that every believer will receive messages from the Spirit. It is a specific promise to the apostles. They were witnesses to all that Jesus had said and done. They had a specific role to provide a first-hand account of Jesus. John, for example, opens his letter by emphasising that "we" apostles heard, saw and touched the Word of life (1 John 1 v 1-3). To ensure that their account is 100% reliable, Jesus promises to send the Spirit. The Spirit would remind them of everything Jesus had said and done. And the Spirit would teach the true meaning of the saving work of Jesus. The true God is the one we see in Jesus and the true Jesus is the one we read about in the testimony of the apostles—the testimony we have in the pages of the New Testament. So the miracles of the apostles that we read about in the book of Acts are key because they confirm their testimony about Jesus and their role as first-hand witnesses. Likewise Paul said, "I persevered in demonstrating among you the marks of a true apostle, including signs, wonders and miracles" (2 Corinthians 12 v 12).

In his life, the words and works of Jesus worked together to bring faith. Jesus said, "Believe me when I say that I am in the Father and the Father is in me; or at least believe on the evidence of the works themselves" (John 14 v 11). Today we find the words and works of Jesus in one place: the apostolic testimony that we find in the New Testament.

Demanding what has already been given

In Matthew 12 v 38 and Luke 11 v 29 the Pharisees demand a sign from Jesus. And still people today demand that God perform a sign. Some unbelievers demand a sign before they will believe. Some Christians believe they have a right to a miracle. But Jesus replies, "A wicked and adulterous generation asks for a sign!" (Matthew 12 v 39). It's wicked to demand a sign because it implies that what God has already provided is not enough. And it's wicked to demand a sign because you're telling God what to do. You're demanding that the Lord of all should act as your personal servant.

Jesus continues, "But none will be given it except the sign of the prophet Jonah" (Matthew 12 v 39). Matthew and Luke's account interpret this in slightly different ways, both illuminating for our discussion of miracles. Matthew's account says, "For as Jonah was three days and three night in the belly of a huge fish, so the Son of Man will be three days and three nights in the heart of the earth" (Matthew 12 v 40). In other words, Jonah's release from the fish after three days is a picture of the resurrection of Jesus after three days. The sign that really matters is the resurrection. Remember, miracles are amazing acts of power through which God reveals his glory and rescues his people. The resurrection is the ultimate sign: it is the ultimate revelation of God's glory and the proof that God's rescue of his people is complete. We don't need anything more than this.

In Luke's account of this story the focus is slightly different. Luke focuses on the preaching of Jonah. "The men of Nineveh will stand up at the judgment with this generation and condemn it, for they repented at the preaching of Jonah; and now something greater than Jonah is here" (Luke 11 v 32). You don't need a bigger rescue from God than the one you've already received in the resurrection—and you don't need a better revelation of God than the revelation you receive in the preaching of God's word.

So the primary purposes of miracles have reached their climax. This is how the writer of Hebrews puts it:

In the past God spoke to our ancestors through the prophets at many times and in various ways, but in these last days he has spoken to us by his Son, whom he appointed heir of all things, and through whom also he made the universe. The Son is the radiance of God's glory and the exact representation of his being, sustaining all things by his powerful word. After he had provided purification for sins, he sat down at the right hand of the Majesty in heaven. *Hebrews 1 v 1-3*

In the past God revealed himself in various ways—including mighty signs and wonders. But now he has revealed himself in his Son. And it's not that Jesus is second best. It's not that we would be better off seeing miracles, but we have to make do with the stories of Jesus. Jesus is the "exact representation" of God's being. God's revelation doesn't get better or clearer than Jesus.

All of God's mighty acts in rescuing his people pointed to the ultimate, final mighty act of salvation—the cross and resurrection of Jesus. And that work is done. That's the significance of Jesus being "sat down" (Hebrews 1 v 3). Jesus sits because his work is complete. And, again, salvation in Jesus is not second best—far from it. A healing might last a lifetime. Resurrection to a new life lasts for ever.

On one occasion, when Jesus was teaching in a home in Capernaum, some friends carried a paralysed man in the hope that Jesus would heal him. Finding the house rammed with people, they created a hole in its mud roof and lowered their friend down to Jesus. "When Jesus saw their faith," we're told, "he said to the paralysed man, 'Son, your sins are forgiven'" (Mark 2 v 5). It's a shocking statement. Those who were there at the time were shocked because only God can forgive sins, so they regarded it as blasphemy. Jesus, however, proves his authority to forgive by then healing the man. The miracle demonstrates his unique identity. But we also find Jesus' words shocking because we think we know what this man needs. There he is, lying in front of Jesus, unable to walk. Surely he needs to be healed. But he has a much bigger need. We all do. We need to be forgiven. Our sin separates us from God and incurs his judgment. A lifetime of paralysis is a terrible plight. But far worse is an eternity in hell.

Miracles are designed to reveal God's glory and save his people. But now the revelation of God is complete in Christ and the Bible. And the salvation of God is also complete in the cross and resurrection. There is, however, one more thing that's required if people are going to be saved and it's something that requires a miracle. And so it is that Jesus promises that we will do miracles, miracles that are even greater than the miracles he performed.

That's the theme of the next chapter...

Chapter 4

What are the greater miracles promised by Jesus?

On the night before he died Jesus told his disciples, "Very truly I tell you, whoever believes in me will do the works I have been doing, and they will do even greater things than these, because I am going to the Father" (John 14 v 12). It looks like a promise that we will do miracles like the miracles Jesus did—perhaps we, too, can walk on water, still storms, and raise the dead.

In fact, though, Jesus has something specific in mind. Jesus has already told us what he means by "greater works" in John 5:

> The Father loves the Son and shows him all he does. Yes, and he will show him even greater works than these, so that you will be amazed. For just as the Father raises the dead and gives them life, even so the Son gives life to whom he is pleased to give it. *John 5 v 20-21*

The greater works take place when Jesus gives eternal life to people. When someone becomes a Christian, they pass from death to life. It's not something they achieve. It's a gift given by Jesus. It's a miracle taking place in their soul.

People are dead in their sins (Ephesians 2 v 1-3). How can that change? They can't change themselves—they're dead. They're as incapable of self-improvement as a corpse. But God works a powerful miracle in them as a result of which they become alive in Christ. They were spiritually blind, but God miraculously opens their eyes to recognise the glory of Christ. They were enemies of God, but God miraculously transforms their affections so that they pursue God. They had hearts of stone, but God miraculously melts their cold hearts and fills them with love. There is no greater miracle. Curing physical blindness is easy compared to curing spiritual blindness. Resuscitating physical bodies is easy compared to granting spiritual life. And God has done it again and again. Forty years ago he did it in me, and he did it in you if you're a Christian.

Not only that, but we get to be involved. This is what Jesus means when he says we will do greater miracles. As we preach the gospel, God grants eternal life. He opens blind eyes and melts cold hearts so that people respond to our message with faith. Here's how Paul puts it in 2 Corinthians:

> The god of this age has blinded the minds of
> unbelievers, so that they cannot see the light of
> the gospel that displays the glory of Christ, who

is the image of God. For what we preach is not ourselves, but Jesus Christ as Lord, and ourselves as your servants for Jesus' sake. For God, who said, "Let light shine out of darkness," made his light shine in our hearts to give us the light of the knowledge of God's glory displayed in the face of Christ.   *2 Corinthians 4 v 4-6*

Here's the problem: people are blinded by Satan to the glory of Christ. That's why they refuse to come to him. Here's our role: we preach Christ. Here's the miracle: God reveals the glory of God in Christ to people so that they entrust themselves to him. Indeed, Paul says the only thing that compares with this moment is the very first creation of the world. Just as God brought light to darkness through his word at creation so now God brings spiritual light to dark hearts through his word. Every conversion is on a par with the act that brought the universe into being! No wonder Jesus calls it a "greater work". This is the miracle that took place in your heart if you're a Christian. And this is the miracle you can perform by speaking of Christ to other people. You can be a miracle worker.

Miracles and mission

Jesus once told a parable. A rich man lived in luxury while at his gate lived a poor beggar named Lazarus. When they died, Lazarus was carried by angels to Abraham's side, but the rich man was in torment in hell. In the parable the rich man sees Abraham with Lazarus at his side and calls on Abraham to send Lazarus to "dip the tip of his finger in water and cool my tongue" (Luke 16 v 24). But this cannot be done because "a great chasm has been set in place" between heaven and hell (v 26). The warning is clear: There is life after death and your eternal future is irrevocably set in this life. In the light of these great truths, we need to see the spiritual danger of money. Money can entice us away from giving our lives to God. Just before he told this parable, Jesus had said, "You cannot serve both God and Money" (Luke 16 v 13).

And that might be that. But Jesus doesn't stop there. The parable has a strange final twist. The rich man says to Abraham:

> "… I beg you, father, send Lazarus to my family, for I have five brothers. Let him warn them, so that they will not also come to this place of torment."
>
> Abraham replied, "They have Moses and the Prophets; let them listen to them."
>
> "No, father Abraham," he said, "but if someone from the dead goes to them, they will repent."
>
> He said to him, "If they do not listen to Moses and the Prophets, they will not be convinced even if someone rises from the dead."   *Luke 16 v 27-31*

The parable is a warning to repent before it's too late and the rich man wants that warning to be heard by his five brothers. But Abraham says they can *already* hear the warning. They have it in "Moses and the Prophets". As we've seen, that was a common way of referring to the Scriptures. All the information we need for salvation is found in the Bible. And it's not as if it's tucked away in the small print. The Bible is one long plea to sinners to turn back to God and find joy, life and hope in Christ. The Bible is God's appeal to us.

But the rich man doesn't think it's enough. He wants more. "No, father Abraham," he said, "but if someone from the dead goes to them, they will repent." He flatly contradicts Abraham. You can see the logic of his position. The Bible is not dramatic enough, not dynamic enough, not exciting enough. But a miracle—that would surely do the job. Someone risen from the dead would convince people.

But Abraham—or rather Jesus as he tells the parable—won't budge. The problem is not any deficiency in the Bible. The problem is that people refuse to listen to its message. And if they ignore the Bible, then they'll ignore someone from the dead as well.

You don't believe it? Consider the other Lazarus. This parable in Luke 16 is the only parable in which Jesus gives someone a name. Why's that? In part, perhaps, it's to give poor Lazarus a dignity that wasn't normally afforded him. You can bet that everyone in town knew the name of the rich man, but hardly anyone would even notice the beggar at his gate. In the story, Jesus reverses this. The rich man is anonymous while Lazarus is named. But it may be that Jesus also wanted to make a link to his friend Lazarus. John 11 describes how this real-life Lazarus died. But Jesus stood before his tomb and cried out, "Lazarus, come out!" And Lazarus came out, still wrapped in his grave clothes.

What happens next? Many people believe in Jesus (John 11 v 45)—just as the rich man in the parable predicted. But the chief priests, Pharisees and Sanhedrin (Jewish court) begin to plot to kill Jesus (John 11 v 46-53). Not only that, they also plot to kill Lazarus—which is a bold move considering he's got a proven record of not staying dead (John 12 v 9-11)! In other words, it's all too possible for people to see a miracle and be *hardened* in their unbelief. That's John's reflection of these events:

> Even after Jesus had performed so many signs in
> their presence, they still would not believe in him.
> This was to fulfil the word of Isaiah the prophet:
> "Lord, who has believed our message and to
> whom has the arm of the Lord been revealed?"
> *John 12 v 37-38*

But, you might say, "OK, some people believed because of the raising of Lazarus and some people were hardened. But I'll take that. That's a positive result. At least some people are believing". But it's more complex than that. The quality of the faith produced by miracles is suspect. John establishes this right at the beginning of his Gospel. After he describes the first "sign" of Jesus—the turning of water into wine (John 2 v 1-12)—John says, "Now while he was in Jerusalem at the Passover Festival, many people saw the signs he was performing and believed in his name. But Jesus would not entrust himself to them, for he knew all people" (John 2 v 23-24). Here are people who "believed" in Jesus, but Jesus didn't trust their faith. It wasn't true faith. Jesus didn't entrust himself to them because they hadn't really entrusted themselves to him. This was fair-weather faith.

It's easy to believe in Jesus when he's performing miracles. "A great crowd of people followed [Jesus]," says John 6 v 2, "because they saw the signs he had performed by healing those who were ill." Things get even better when this crowd witnesses Jesus feed 5,000+ people using just five loaves and two fish. "After the people saw the sign Jesus performed, they began to say, 'Surely this is the Prophet who is to come into the world'" (John 6 v 14). But then Jesus starts talking about how he himself is the bread of life (John 6 v 25-59). What really matters is not getting free bread but trusting Jesus for eternal life. What we really need to do, he says, is feed on his body and blood through faith. As a result of this teaching, "from this time many of his disciples turned back and no longer followed him" (John 6 v 66). Everyone likes the idea of free stuff and quick solutions. But what about when suffering comes?

Jesus talks about this in the parable of the sower. The seed that fell on rocky ground represents those "who receive the word with joy when they hear it, but they have no root. These believe for a while, but in the time of testing they fall away" (Luke 8 v 13). Compare this to the faith of the disciples. Just before John tells us that Jesus did not trust faith based on miracles, he writes:

The Jews then responded to [Jesus], "What sign can you show us to prove your authority to do all this?"

Jesus answered them, "Destroy this temple, and I will raise it again in three days."

They replied, "It has taken forty-six years to build this temple, and you are going to raise it in three days?" But the temple he had spoken of was his body. After he was raised from the dead, his disciples recalled what he had said. Then they believed the Scripture and the words that Jesus had spoken.
John 2 v 18-22

The disciples' faith was based on "Scripture and the words that Jesus had spoken". And these people did not fall away when "the time of testing" came (Luke 8 v 13). Instead, they became the apostles who led the church in the face of persecution.

Don't mistake what I'm saying. I'm not against miracles. Indeed, I think they do sometimes play a role in people coming to Christ. But here's the key point: *In mission the Bible is necessary and sufficient while miracles are neither necessary nor sufficient.*

In other words, we need the Bible to do mission. I don't mean we need to give everyone a physical copy of the Bible. But we do need to speak God's word and that word must be derived and controlled by the Bible. "Faith comes from hearing the message, and the message is heard through the word about Christ" (Romans 10 v 17). You don't need to carry a Bible around with you every time you do evangelism. But you do need to ensure the words you proclaim to people are words based on the message of the Scriptures.

So the Bible is necessary. But it's also *sufficient* when the Holy Spirit works through the words to open blind eyes. You don't need anything else. If you just proclaim words based on the words of the Scriptures, then God can use this to save people. So the Bible is both necessary and sufficient.

In contrast, miracles are neither necessary nor sufficient. Sometimes they may play a role in someone's story of conversion. But people can be saved without seeing a miracle, and seeing a miracle is never enough—people also need to hear the message of Christ crucified.

Miracles and the work of Satan

Not every miracle is a sign that God is at work. We are right to be cautious and careful about miraculous claims. Modern science recognises the power of the mind to affect the body. For example, placebos can cure ailments even though they contain no active ingredients. But there may also be more sinister factors at work in some miracles.

The magicians of Egypt replicated some of the miracles of Moses "by their secret arts" (Exodus 7 v 11, 22; 8 v 7). A man called Simon practised sorcery and amazed the people of Samaria (Acts 8 v 9-11) while a slave girl in Philippi was able profitably to predict the future until Paul commanded a spirit to leave her (Acts 16 v 16-18). Paul warns, "The coming of the lawless one will be in accordance with how Satan works. He will use all sorts of displays of power through signs and wonders that serve the lie, and all the ways that wickedness deceives those who are perishing" (2 Thessalonians 2 v 9-10; see also Revelation 13 v 11-14).

Satan and his demons are able to perform miracles. This means miracles are not a sure sign that someone is from God. "Satan himself," warns Paul in 2 Corinthians 11 v 14, "masquerades as an angel of light". Some people who appear to be powerful men or women of God can be charlatans or worse. Jesus himself warns:

> Many will say to me on that day, "Lord, Lord, did we not prophesy in your name and in your name drive out demons and in your name perform many miracles?" Then I will tell them plainly, "I never knew you. Away from me, you evildoers!"
>
> *Matthew 7 v 22-23*

Genuine miracles point to Jesus. In contrast, all too often with those who make miracles a feature of their ministry the miracles end up pointing to the miracle-worker. Or the focus is on the miracles rather than on Jesus. "God did extraordinary miracles through Paul" (Acts 19 v 11). But Paul was determined to ensure the focus of his ministry was "Christ and him crucified" (1 Corinthians 2 v 2). What must be central is the preaching of the cross. Where the cross is not front and centre, something is badly wrong.

The pattern of miracles today

The link between the role of miracles in the Bible and the role of the Bible today enables us to explain the pattern of miracles today.

1. On the frontline of mission

We often see more miracles on the front-line of mission and this should not surprise us. Even within the New Testament we see this (John 4 v 29; Acts 5 v 12-16; 8 v 6-8; 9 v 35). Miracles abound when the gospel enters new territory. John Stott says, "Especially on the frontiers of mission, where a power-encounter may be needed to demonstrate the lordship of Christ, miracles have been and are being reported".[15]

There are a number of things that make people more inclined to pay attention to the Christian message: the lives of Christians (Titus 2 v 9-10); our response to persecution (1 Peter 2 v 11-12); the community life of the church (John 13 v 35; 1 Peter 3 v 8-15); the worship of the gathered congregation (1 Corinthians 14 v 23-25). But these things are largely absent where a church has not yet been formed. In such contexts, it may be that miracles are more common.

2. Where the Bible is absent

Another key factor will be the absence of the Bible. As we have seen, we encounter the words and works of Jesus through the apostolic testimony in the New Testament. But on the frontline of mission there may be no copies of the New Testament, maybe even no translation of the Bible in the local language. In such contexts, it may be that miracles play a more significant role.

---

15 John Stott in David Edwards with John Stott, *Essentials: A Liberal-Evangelical Dialogue* (Hodder & Stoughton, 1988), p 219.

3. When the occult is strong

As we have seen, it seems that Satan's primary approach in the west at the moment is to spread the lie of materialism, and, to this end, overt Satanic activity is uncommon. In this context, our spiritual warfare is to confront this lie by proclaiming the truth. But where people are involved in Satanic or occult activity, we can expect a different type of confrontation between the people of God and the agents of Satan—one that might involve some form of miraculous release from Satan's grip.

There is one point in the story of Acts where Luke describes the miracles being performed as "extraordinary". Even by the standards of the early apostolic period, these miracles were exceptional. Luke says, "God did extraordinary miracles through Paul, so that even handkerchiefs or aprons that had touched him were taken to those who were ill, and their illnesses were cured and the evil spirits left them" (Acts 19 v 11-12). The striking thing is that these took place in Ephesus, a notorious centre for occult activity. Luke himself highlights this very point. He describes a group of seven itinerant Jewish exorcists trying to evoke the name of Jesus but being overpowered by the evil spirit (Acts 19 v 13-17). As a result, many people confessed their occult practices. Those who had practiced "sorcery" brought their books of spells and burnt them in a public bonfire—sending items valued at around 50,000 silver coins up in smoke (Acts 19 v 18-19). Here was a culture deeply entwined with occult practices and this is the context in which Paul did extraordinary miracles. Yet still the focus is on the word of God, for Luke draws this confrontation to a close with the words, "In this way the word of the Lord spread widely and grew in power" (Acts 19 v 20).

4. When believers are immature

John Frame also suggests that God often provides for young believers in more direct and miraculous ways.[16] A parent closely watches a small child and often intervenes in a direct way to prevent them from coming to harm. The child strays near the road and the parent pulls them out of danger. The child feels hungry and the parent spoons food into their mouth. In a similar way, perhaps, God intervenes more directly in the lives of young believers. He keeps them from danger more times than perhaps they realise. But his intent is that they grow and mature. He wants them to learn to avoid temptation and trust him in adversity.

So God may directly intervene less as Christians mature. His interventions become geared towards shaping the Christian's heart rather than changing their circumstances. Indeed, God may use suffering and unanswered prayer to refine our faith. Frame concludes:

> *When young Christians become more mature, they often wonder why such things happen to them less often or not at all. They worry that their faith has grown dim, because they don't see as many supernatural events in their lives. That may be so, but it may also be the case that in their individual*

---

16 John Frame, *The Doctrine of God* (P&R, 2012), p 276.

lives, as often in Scripture, the extraordinary has been a preparation for the ordinary.[17]

Our compassionate God

On one occasion, Jesus spends an evening healing many people. The following morning the disciples come to find him because everyone is looking for him. People are queuing up, as it were, to see a miracle. But Jesus avoids the crowds. "Let us go somewhere else," he says, "to the nearby villages—so that I can preach there also. That is why I have come" (Mark 1 v 38). The next thing that happens is that Jesus meets a man with leprosy who says, "If you are willing, you can make me clean" (Mark 1 v 40). It's an odd thing to say. If the man had met me, he might have said, "If you are able, you would make me clean". He would doubt my ability. But there are no doubts about the ability of Jesus. What's in doubt is his willingness because he has just avoided the miracle-seeking crowds so that he can devote himself to preaching. Preaching is his priority and miracles are a distraction. So what happens? "Moved with pity, he stretched out his hand and touched him and said to him, 'I will; be clean'" (Mark 1 v 41, ESV). Preaching is Jesus' priority, but he still performs a miracle because he is filled with compassion.

The same is true today. The primary purpose for miracles is to reveal God's glory and rescue his people. These purposes have come to a climax in the Lord Jesus Christ and the record of his work in the New Testament. God

---

17 John Frame, *The Doctrine of God* (P&R, 2012), p 276.

is still active in his world. He is still a God who is full of compassion. So he does intervene through miracles to provide for his people. But he does so less often now that the primary purpose of miracles has been fulfilled. We certainly don't need to worry if we're not seeing many miracles in our lives or our churches. What matters is that we have faith in the resurrection of Jesus, which is the ultimate sign and the promise of eternal life.

What this looks like in daily life we will explore in the next chapter.

Should we hold healing services?

I once attended a "healing meeting" where prayer for miracles was the focus of the meeting. Clearly the success of such occasions depends on whether miracles actually happen and so the pressure is on to deliver. In the meeting I attended, people's expectations were whipped up until some kind of response became inevitable. I'm afraid, though, I was left very sceptical about whether there were lasting results. Certainly there was no sign of spiritual fruit. The focus was all on the man on the stage rather than the man of the cross. If this is what you mean by healing meetings, then I would definitely avoid them.

But it doesn't have to be like this.

I used to be part of a church in which during communion people were invited to go to a side chapel if they wanted someone to pray with them for healing. It was not showy—it happened off to the side, out of sight. The focus of the service was on the cross: the message of the cross was preached and then the message of the cross was embodied in bread and wine.

All the churches of which I've been involved have had times when we've called a special prayer meeting to pray for a crisis—a child diagnosed with a brain tumour, a culmination of events that have added up to a sense of spiritual attack, a crisis in the life of the church. In each case we have come together to pray for a miracle.

But we have also prayed for persevering faith and that God would be glorified whatever the outcome. We have tried to pray with gospel priorities and an eternal perspective. In one case, we agreed that our priority would be not so much that a dying woman would be healed, but that her witness would be bright in the face of death, especially to her unconverted children. And our prayers were answered: she had a profound impact on the hospital staff who cared for and her daughter was converted through her funeral.

John Stott says of the miracles of Jesus, "They were never performed selfishly or senselessly. Their purpose was not to show off or to compel submission. There were not so much demonstrations of physical power as illustrations of moral authority. They were in fact the acted parables of Jesus."[18]

---

18 John Stott, Basic Christianity, IVP, second edition, 1971, 32.

Chapter 5

Can I pray for a miracle?

Can I pray for a miracle? Yes. Miracles may not happen today in the way they did in the ministry of Jesus and the apostles. But they do happen today. God is a compassionate Father who is powerfully involved in his world and who invites us to bring our cares to him. John Stott writes:

> *Those of us who believe (as I do) that the major function of miracles no longer exists, because we are not living in a fresh epoch of revelation or redemption, and that therefore we have no liberty to expect miracles to occur with the frequency with which they occurred in such epochs, should nevertheless be entirely open to them. We believe that God the Creator is free, sovereign and powerful. We must not attempt to domesticate God, or dictate to him what he is allowed to do.*[19]

---

19 John Stott in David Edwards with John Stott, *Essentials: A Liberal-Evangelical Dialogue* (Hodder and Stoughton, 1988), p 218-219.

Nevertheless, we need to view our desire for a miracle in the wider context of God's purposes. Miracles are not the central focus of walking with God. Let's explore what this might mean in practice.

Miracles and the power of faith

What do you need to do to see a miracle? It turns out the answer is: very little.

Some Christians talk as if you need to screw up your faith and lay claim to this specific miracle. Unless you believe it will happen, they imply, then it won't happen. Some even talk as if God is limited by our faith—or lack of faith. They point to Mark 6 v 5-6 where Jesus visits his home town of Nazareth and we're told, "He could not do any miracles there, except lay his hands on a few people who were ill and heal them. He was amazed at their lack of faith".

But the problem here is not that Jesus was constrained by a lack of faith. We can't limit God. It's rather that doing more miracles would have hardened people's opposition to him. We've already seen how miracles sometimes made people more resolute in their opposition to Jesus. This was the attitude Jesus found in his home town. So it was his mercy that prevented him from performing more miracles, not his impotency. His miracles would have compounded their guilt. In other places, it seems, miracles had made things worse, for Jesus says elsewhere, "If I had not done among them the works no one else did, they would not be guilty of sin. As it is, they have seen, and yet they have hated both me and my Father" (John 15 v 24).

You do need to believe that God is a loving Father who hears his children's cries—otherwise you won't bother calling out to him in prayer. But you don't need to believe that this specific miracle will happen. You don't need to believe your cancer will definitely be healed in order for your cancer to be healed. You don't need to believe you will receive a gift out of the blue in order to receive a gift out of the blue. In fact, you *can't* know for sure that things will happen. Maybe it will prove to be God's will to perform a miracle, but maybe it won't.

In fact, the experience of the early church suggests you don't even really need to believe God *could* perform the miracle for which you're asking—never mind believing he *will* do so. When Peter was thrown in prison, the church gathered to pray for his release. In the night, an angel came, freed Peter from his manacles, opened the gates of the prison and led Peter out. In the most dramatic fashion, God answered the prayers of the church. What happened next is fascinating. Peter turns up at the prayer meeting organised to pray for his release.

Peter knocked at the outer entrance, and a servant named Rhoda came to answer the door. When she recognised Peter's voice, she was so overjoyed she ran back without opening it and exclaimed, "Peter is at the door!"

"You're out of your mind," they told her. When she kept insisting that it was so, they said, "It must be his angel."

> But Peter kept on knocking, and when they
> opened the door and saw him, they were
> astonished.   *Acts 12 v 13-16*

The church cannot believe it's Peter. After all, he was locked up in prison. But remember what they're doing as these events unfold: they're praying for his release. Their prayer is answered, but they can't believe it—even with Peter knocking on the door. They have faith in God—that's why they gather to pray. But clearly they don't believe a miracle will happen. Nevertheless, a miracle does happen.

When Jesus turns up after Lazarus has died, Martha and Mary are clearly disappointed that, as far as they're concerned, Jesus has arrived too late. They have faith. They believe that Jesus could have cured their brother. "Lord, if you had been here," they both say, "my brother would not have died" (John 11 v 21, 32). What neither of them believes is that Jesus will raise their brother from the tomb. Even when Jesus gives Martha a pretty big hint that this is what he's going to do, Martha interprets it as a reference to the resurrection at the end of time (John 11 v 23-24). Yet, despite the fact that they're not anticipating Lazarus to come back from the dead, that's what happens (John 11 v 38-44).

Let's sum this up.

- You *can* have faith that God *can* perform a miracle—because God is powerfully involved in his world.

- You *can't* have faith that God *will* perform a miracle—because God doesn't always or even often perform miracles.

- You *don't need* to have faith that God *can* or *will* perform a miracle—because God is not dependent on your faith.

This is so encouraging. We can be left fearing that whether a miracle happens or not is down to us. Only if we can summon up enough faith, we suppose, can we "unleash" the power of God. But God's power is not on "leash" and you're not holding its fastener! Whether a miracle happens or not is down to the wisdom of God. And that means the issue is in safe hands.

Miracles and the purposes of God

God is a Father who loves his children and cares for them. But his great plan for our life is that we might be conformed to his Son. And sometimes he uses suffering to achieve this purpose. As we look to God, as we pray for one another, as we pray with one another, we need to keep this wider perspective in view.

> We also glory in our sufferings, because we know that suffering produces perseverance; perseverance, character; and character, hope. And hope does not put us to shame, because God's love has been poured out into our hearts through the Holy Spirit, who has been given to us.
>
> *Romans 5 v 3-5*

Consider it pure joy, my brothers and sisters, whenever you face trials of many kinds, because you know that the testing of your faith produces perseverance. Let perseverance finish its work so that you may be mature and complete, not lacking anything.

James 1 v 2-4

In ... this [living hope] you greatly rejoice, though now for a little while you may have had to suffer grief in all kinds of trials. These have come so that the proven genuineness of your faith—of greater worth than gold, which perishes even though refined by fire—may result in praise, glory and honour when Jesus Christ is revealed.

1 Peter 1 v 6-7

Suffering, trials, grief. You might well pray for a miracle to bring sufferings, trials and grief to an end. But consider how God uses them. In God's hands the end result can be perseverance, character, hope, love, maturity, proof, purity along with praise, glory and honour for Jesus. These things are not second best! If a miracle does not take place and what you get instead are perseverance, character, hope, love, maturity, proof, purity and glory then you are not being hard done by.

If God miraculously heals you, it is because he is compassionate. But if God does not heal you, he is still compassionate, he is still showing compassion towards you and he is still being good to you.

So how should we pray for one another? Paul gives a model in Colossians 1:

⁹ We continually ask God to fill you with the knowledge of his will through all the wisdom and understanding that the Spirit gives, ¹⁰ so that you may live a life worthy of the Lord and please him in every way: bearing fruit in every good work, growing in the knowledge of God, ¹¹ being strengthened with all power according to his glorious might so that you may have great endurance and patience, ¹² and giving joyful thanks to the Father, who has qualified you to share in the inheritance of his holy people in the kingdom of light. *Colossians 1 v 9-12*

The heart of Paul's prayer is a request for knowledge of God's will: "We continually ask God to fill you with the knowledge of his will through all the wisdom and understanding that the Spirit gives" (v 9). He defines what this means in verse 10 when he prays for "the knowledge of his will … so that you may live a life worthy of the Lord and please him in every way". The will of God is the way of life that pleases God, a life that reflects his character and his purposes. Paul wants the Colossians to have such a good knowledge of God's character, priorities and word that in any given situation they'll know what it is that will please God.

The knowledge for which Paul prays has a goal: a life worthy of the Lord. "We continually ask God to fill you with the knowledge of his will … so that you may live a life worthy of the Lord and please him in every way" (v 9-10). Just as in many cultures it's important to preserve the honour of the family, so Paul wants us to act in a way that brings honour to Christ. Our lives are to be beautiful, living testimonies to Christ. Paul expands this goal by describing four characteristics of a life that honours Jesus: bearing fruit (v 10), growing in knowledge (v 10), being strengthened to endure (v 11), and giving thanks (v 12).

The third of these four characteristics is significant for our purposes: "being strengthened with all power according to his glorious might so that you may have great endurance and patience" (v 11). Paul prays that the Christians might be strengthened with *all* power. That sounds exciting. It's not just "power", it's "all power". It's not "might", it's "glorious might".

At this point some people might start to think we're promised miracles, success, victory, healing and prosperity. But Paul is also very specific about the *purpose* of this power within us. He prays for power not to do mighty and miraculous works, but *"so that you may have great endurance and patience"*. In other words, we pray for power to stick at the task of Christian service while we wait patiently for Christ's return. The world always looks for quick solutions and instant success. But Christians are called to endure. And for this we need God's power. We need God's power so we can be joyful in suffering and sickness. We need God's power so we can go on loving when rebuffed or mistreated. We need God's power so we can trust God when the road gets rough.

What are the requests you commonly make in prayer? It's all too easy for us to pray for good health, guidance for decisions and successful job interviews. As one church leader put it to me once, our prayer meetings sound too much like a hospital waiting list. But just imagine how different it would be if our prayers lined up with Paul's prayer here in Colossians 1. We would be going beyond the surface and addressing what really matters. It would be real spiritual work. We would be going deep—deep for ourselves, deep for one another.

I can tell you what it would sound like. It would sound like Epaphras. In Colossians 4 v 12 Paul writes:

> Epaphras, who is one of you and a servant of Christ Jesus, sends greetings. He is always wrestling in prayer for you, that you may stand firm in all the will of God, mature and fully assured.
>
> *Colossians 4 v 12*

By all means pray for health, safety and success. But remember that all things are just passing. We can and should pray about anything and everything. God invites us to cast our anxieties on him (1 Peter 5 v 7). But let's pray for anything and everything with *gospel* priorities. Let's pray for anything and everything from an eternal perspective. Let's pray that we "may stand firm in all the will of God, mature and fully assured".

Miracles and the hope of the resurrection

It is my conviction that often Christians pray for a miracle not because their faith is strong, but because it is weak. Perhaps that surprises you. Here's what I mean. I find it striking how often Christians treat death as a tragedy. I say this with caution because I've not yet had to face it personally. But I have known many Christians who embraced the prospect of dying without fear because they were full of faith in Christ and therefore full of the hope of glory. They may not have looked forward to the process of dying, but they did not shrink from death itself.

In contrast other Christians seem to regard death as the worst possible outcome and so they pray desperately for a miracle. A miracle seems to be their only hope. God is a loving Father, they reason, and so surely he will rescue his child from death.

But, of course, God *has* rescued his children from death. He did so by sending his Son to die in our place and raising him up to give us new life. The resurrection is our hope, our true hope, our final hope.

"If the dead are not raised at all," Paul asks in 1 Corinthians 15 v 29-32, "… why do we endanger ourselves every hour? I face death every day—yes, just as surely as I boast about you in Christ Jesus our Lord. If I fought wild beasts in Ephesus with no more than human hopes, what have I gained?" Paul risks his life for the gospel. Why? Because he believes the dead are raised. He believes there is a life after death and for him that will mean eternal life with Christ. His whole perspective on life—his sufferings, his risks, his sacrifice—is shaped by his big vision of God's eternal purposes.

"For to me, to live is Christ and to die is gain." So says Paul in Philippians 1 v 21. At this point death is a real prospect for him. He's in prison and facing martyrdom. So this is not a grand, empty statement. This is the statement of a man staring death in the face. But for Paul "to live is Christ". Christ is the love of his life, his one great preoccupation, his guiding purpose and his ultimate joy. So what will death mean for Paul? Seeing Christ face to face. And that will be glorious. Death is painful because it separates us from what we love. But if what we love most is Christ then death is gain.

Yet all too often Christians pray for a miraculous healing because they do not believe death "is gain". And that presumably is because for them to live is not Christ. Their pursuit for a miracle looks faith-filled, but in reality it's faith-deficient.

In the end every prayer for a miracle is answered in the new creation. In the new earth God "will wipe every tear from their eyes. There will be no more death or mourning or crying or pain, for the old order of things has passed away" (Revelation 21 v 4). In the end every child of God is healed, every child of God is released, every child of God finds peace, every child of God enjoys glory.

John Hooper, a Protestant during the reign of Mary Tudor, was facing martyrdom. He was urged by a friend to renounce the faith. "Life is sweet, death is bitter," his friend told him. Hooper replied, "Eternal life is more sweet, eternal death is more bitter".

What can I say to a child about praying for healing?

Sooner or later, our children will come across someone who is seriously ill or dying. Should we encourage them to pray for healing for that person? And how can we explain it if God's answer to their prayers seems to be "No"? Here's a very helpful answer from Lauren Chandler, who is the wife of American pastor Matt Chandler and the author of the children's storybook, *Goodbye to Goodbyes*:

> *Death is hard to talk to children about. Because it is both scary and abstract, it is hard for children to really understand. So having a story to tell them—whether it's a time in their lives before it has become super-personal for them; or because, sadly, they're now in the midst of dealing with grief; or even when they're looking back on loss—is really helpful. I'm grateful, from personal experience with my kids, that the Bible graciously provides us with one.*
>
> *The story of Lazarus in John 11 teaches children that death does happen, that Jesus knows what grief is like, and that the gospel makes our experience of both grief and of death completely different.*
>
> *Our family went through a season of suffering with Matt when he was diagnosed with a malignant brain tumour. The kids were so young—6, 2 and a baby—and it felt like I was just about keeping my head above water. How could I help my kids process it all?*

Reading the story of Lazarus ministered to me greatly in those painful days. Jesus knew exactly what he was going to do—he was going to raise Lazarus—but in the moment that he saw Mary and Martha, he still entered into their grief. He went all in. He wept with them. This brought me great comfort, because when you're in the midst of a trial like that, there's no guarantee what God will do. Will healing be brought on this side, or will it be on the other side? Will we ever get back to "normal"?

I felt the compassion and empathy of Christ in that moment, and it gave me the confidence to say to the kids, "No matter what happens, Jesus is with us. He's sad with us. And one way or another, Dad will get healing. He will be whole on this side of death, or the next".[20]

This approach is so helpful when we pray for the healing of a believer. Will God heal them? Yes. He may choose to heal them on this side of death, maybe even in a wonderful way that can only be a miracle. But if not, we can have complete certainty that he will heal them beyond death, where "there will be no more death or mourning or crying or pain" (Revelation 21 v 4). The timing and method are in the Lord's hands, and all the glory will go to him.

---

20 https://www.thegoodbook.co.uk/blog/ interestingthoughts/2019/01/29/how-to-talk-to-your-children- about-death/ (accessed on 11 April 2019).

Miracles that point to the truth

At the beginning of this book, I described how a grieving lady asked me whether she could pray for a miracle for her dying friend. Many of us have been in a similar position—longing for the Lord to heal a loved one but not sure how to pray or what to expect.

As we've worked through this book, we have seen that the God of the Bible is a God of miracles. The Bible tells us that he has performed miracles in the past (chapter 1) and can still do so today (chapter 2). We've recognised that he performs fewer miracles today than he did in biblical times and considered why that is (chapter 3). And we've unpacked what Jesus meant when he said his followers would perform "greater miracles" than him (chapter 4).

We've seen that God's purposes can be fulfilled through miracles. But God's purposes can also be fulfilled through natural causes. We have an always-Lord; not an occasional-Lord.

We've also seen that miracles are designed to reveal God's glory and save his people. But now the revelation of God is complete in Christ and the Bible. And the salvation of God is also complete in the cross and resurrection.

So where does that leave us? Can we pray for a miracle? Yes, we can. Can the Lord answer that prayer in a miraculous way? Yes, he can. But should we expect him to do so? Probably not. And can we demand that he do so? Certainly never. Miracles are possible but not probable. The Lord can and does still perform miracles today, but that is not his normal way of working.

The New Testament miracles pointed to the truth about the Lord Jesus, our Saviour. Many of those miracles were seen by eye-witnesses who wrote them down for us so that they point us to the truth about Jesus too. We don't need further miracles—everything we need in order to know who Jesus is and why he came is already revealed in Scripture (Hebrews 1 v 1-3).

Of course, sometimes the Lord does something miraculous anyway, and we can rejoice in his kindness when he does. But his ultimate kindness has already been shown in the coming of his Son. And we will experience the ultimate healing when we join him in the new creation.

thegoodbook
COMPANY

BIBLICAL | RELEVANT | ACCESSIBLE

At The Good Book Company, we are dedicated to helping Christians and local churches grow. We believe that God's growth process always starts with hearing clearly what he has said to us through his timeless word—the Bible.

Ever since we opened our doors in 1991, we have been striving to produce Bible-based resources that bring glory to God. We have grown to become an international provider of user-friendly resources to the Christian community, with believers of all backgrounds and denominations using our books, Bible studies, devotionals, evangelistic resources, and DVD-based courses.

We want to equip ordinary Christians to live for Christ day by day, and churches to grow in their knowledge of God, their love for one another, and the effectiveness of their outreach.

Call us for a discussion of your needs or visit one of our local websites for more information on the resources and services we provide.

Your friends at The Good Book Company

thegoodbook.com | thegoodbook.co.uk
thegoodbook.com.au | thegoodbook.co.nz
thegoodbook.co.in